How to Talk ♥ to Girls

BY ALEC GREVEN

ILLUSTRATIONS BY KEI ACEDERA

HarperCollins *Children's Books*

First published in the UK by HarperCollins Children's Books

How to Talk to Girls
Text copyright © 2008 by Alec Greven
Illustrations copyright © 2008 by Kei Acedera

ISBN 978-0-00-731699-1

Typography by Ray Shappell
1 3 5 7 9 10 8 6 4 2

CONTENTS

INTRODUCTION

Are you shy? Do you have a crush on a girl?
Is the girl you like just too pretty for your eyes?
Do you know what to say to a girl to make her like you?

What are you waiting for?
If you are a boy who needs help getting girls,
this book has all the answers!

*By the way, all statistics in this book are based on
my observations at Soaring Hawk Elementary School.
They aren't worldwide.
I would have to do a lot more research for that.*

Okay, let's get going!

CHAPTER ONE

The Facts of Life

{ Life is hard, move on! }

Sometimes, you get a girl to like you, then she ditches you.

Life is hard, move on!

TIP: *About 73 percent of regular girls ditch boys;*
98 percent of pretty girls ditch boys.

Or sometimes it just doesn't work out.

I had a crush on a girl in preschool.
Then my family had to move,
so I had to let her wash out of my mind.

You also have to be aware that girls win most of the arguments and have most of the power. If you know that now, things might be easier.

Finally, if you try for too many girls, you will have jealousy issues and might end up with nobody.
It is really best to go for just one.

If you do get a girl to like you, that is victory.
Winning victory is a dream for most boys,
but it is very rare.

What does it take to win victory?

Read on and find out!

CHAPTER TWO

Crushes

{ *A crush is like a love disease. It can drive you mad.* }

Many boys get crushes on girls.
But it can be very hard to get a girl to like you.
Sometimes it takes years!
Whatever happens, just don't act desperate.
Girls don't like desperate boys.

So what do you do if you have a crush on a girl?
You need to get her to like you.

You can also show off a skill, like playing
soccer or anything else that you are good at.

TIP: *To get a girl to like you, talk to her and get to know her.*

If you are in elementary school, try to get a girl
to like you, not to *love* you.
Wait until middle school to try to get her to love you.
Otherwise, you have to hold on to her for a long time
and that would be very hard.

TIP: *Most boys in elementary school can hold on to a girl*
for only 30 days.

Many boys who have crushes don't know how to act around a girl.
Some boys tease girls they like and are mean to them.
Some boys say silly things to girls and act goofy.
Some boys think they are acting cool by showing off.
This is not a good approach.

The right thing to do when you have a crush is:

- ✓ Never show off too much
- ✓ Don't be silly and goofy
- ✓ Control your hyperness (cut down on sugar if you need to)
- ✓ Make sure you have good friends who won't try to take the girl you like.

Finally, you have to be able to get over a crush
if it doesn't work out.
A crush is like a love disease.
It can drive you mad.

Try not to let it get you down.

CHAPTER THREE

There's a Girl for Every Boy

{ You are like a magnet and girls are the metal. }

Girls are everywhere.
It is not hard to find a girl.
The trick is, how do you find the right girl for you?

Many boys go for the pretty girls.
It is easy to spot pretty girls because they have the big earrings,
fancy dresses, and all the jewelry.

Use caution!
When you see a pretty girl, don't let her tractor beam pull you in.

Pretty girls are like cars that need a lot of oil.
And if you fail with a pretty girl, it mostly drives you crazy.
If you are really confident, go for it!

But the best choice for most boys is a regular girl.
Remember, some pretty girls are coldhearted when it comes to boys.

Don't let them get to you.

Some girls are wild.

Most girls like polite boys – but not the wild girls.
If the girl you like is wild, then act just like her.

Some girls are talkative. Some girls are shy.

Go for a talkative girl if you are shy.
Then you only have to say one sentence,
and she will do the rest of the talking.

Girls always like the smart boys.

What if you were the smartest kid in the class?
Girls would be prowling at your feet.
Pick one and skip along.

If you try to go out with all of them, it just gets crazy!

If you are the smartest kid in the class, you are like a magnet and girls are the metal.

CHAPTER FOUR

How to Get a Girl's Attention

{ Most girls don't like show-offs. }

Do you think that attracting a girl's attention means
flapping your arms like a chicken and making noise?
No way.
You'll be ditched if you do that.

Attention is a very important way to get girls.
But you need to be careful.

Getting a girl's attention is a very hard thing and it takes a lot of work.

Concentrate now, because this is where some boys make mistakes.
You want the girl to notice you.
But you don't want to draw too much attention to yourself or she will think you are a crazy madman who doesn't even know where his own brain is.

To get attention, you might want to show off a skill.
But don't be a show-off.
Most girls don't like show-offs.

Don't brag or she will ditch you.

Another thing *not* to do is be a class clown.
This is not a good way to get a girl's attention.
Class clowns disrupt the whole class.
Very few class clowns get girls to like them.
And class clowns never make a living.

Jokes are good as long as they are not during class.

Class clowns never make a good love story with a girl,
if you catch my drift.

CHAPTER FIVE

What to Say to Girls

{ *If she says "hi" back, you are off to a good start.* }

If you want to start a conversation with a girl,
first you have to say something like "hi."

If she says "hi" back, you are off to a good start.

It's good to let the girl start off the conversation.
You want her to talk. If she doesn't talk, then you have to.

Be friendly. Act calm and don't be nervous.
Don't say anything mean. Ask her a question
and then you are off!

Some good questions to ask are:
✓ "Did you see that episode of _____?"
✓ "I heard you went to _____. What did you do?"

If she doesn't want to talk to you, then either she is shy
or she doesn't like you. You might want to get out of there
and try another day.

If she doesn't like you, don't worry, it happens.

Another good way to start a conversation is to get the girl's phone number (if your mom lets you call girls).

If the girl doesn't give you her phone number or
if she gives you the wrong number, then she doesn't like you and you should move on.

What if you are *really* shy?
I don't know much about this,
but I will try to give you some ideas.

Pick a girl in the class. Ask her to be your friend.
That's a good way to start.

If you have behavior problems, copy a boy
you think is cool and act exactly like him.

CHAPTER SIX

Compliments, Flowers, and Other Things

{ *If you like a girl, comb your hair and don't wear sweats.* }

It is good to give a girl compliments.
Don't go crazy with them, though.
Then you look like you are trying too hard.
Try to act normal.
Many girls like flowers.

It is also good to give gifts.
They don't have to be big.
Try to find out what she likes before
you give her something.
You should go around to her friends to get ideas.
And I wouldn't do flowers and gifts until
you are older, like in middle school,
because it seems weird in elementary school.
Unless you go to a school dance.

Then you could buy her something they have for sale,
like a raffle ticket or a carnation.

In elementary school some kids give notes. But that is risky.
If the note is intercepted, then the girl might ditch you out
of embarrassment.

If you like a girl, comb your hair and don't wear sweats.
You don't have to try too hard, but just try to look kind of clean.

TIP: *Your mom likes you to always be clean, and she is a girl.*

If you are interested in dating, you have to be kind of old –
like fifteen or sixteen if it is okay with your parents.

Dating is like going to dinner together without your
parents coming along.

In elementary school you don't date.
You might hang out at school, or at a party or a dance.
You might talk and play at recess, or sit together at lunch.

When you hang out, try not to say anything inappropriate.
Only make jokes that she would like. Try to focus.
You have to say the right things at the right time.
And then you hope that she agrees with you.

Finally, if you go somewhere, like to a dance or party, dress nicely.
If not, you might end up in a spot of trouble.

CHAPTER SEVEN

Success!

{ *If you do win victory with a girl, don't cheer in front of her.* }

As I said before, winning victory is a dream for most boys. Winning victory means the girl you like likes you back.

It is very rare, but if you do win victory with a girl, don't cheer in front of her or it's a straightaway ditch.

TIP: *Go somewhere private, then knock your head off and cheer.*

It's pretty hard to get a girl to like you.
But if you do win victory, don't stop.

To keep a girl liking you:
- ✓ Be friendly
- ✓ Look clean
- ✓ Act normal—don't try to be *too* cool
- ✓ Don't act goofy
- ✓ Show off a skill, but don't be a show-off
- ✓ Give compliments
- ✓ Don't brag

. . . or else you'll have to start all over!

Now don't scream if you can't get the girl even after you've tried everything. If it doesn't work out, just let it go.

Whatever happens, don't let it make you crazy.

That's it. I am all out of ideas.
Good-bye! Good luck!

ACKNOWLEDGMENTS

Thank You!

To my family: Mom, Dad, Tyler, and Keira

And to the people who caused a chain reaction and helped me so much:

Anna Dupree

Laura Brinkman

Laura Alfano

Janice Perry

The staff of Soaring Hawk Elementary School

My class and friends (including Kane, who moved away)

Regina and Debbie at Ambiance Salon

Kim Christiansen and Kirk Montgomery

Ellen DeGeneres

ExactBind Rocky Mountain

HarperCollins Children's Books

And you, the reader, for buying my book!

—Alec